IN THE HALF LIGHT
OF A DYING DAY

BY THE SAME AUTHOR

POETRY

Whether the Will is Free
Crossing the Bar
Quesada
Walking Westward
Geographies
Poems of a Decade
Paris
Between
Voices
Straw into Gold
The Right Thing
Dog
The Red Tram
The Black River
Collected Poems, 1951–2006
The Yellow Buoy: Poems 2007–2012
In the Mirror, and Dancing
That Derrida Whom I Derided Died:
    Poems 2013–2017
Say I Do This: Poems 2018–2022

FICTION

Smith's Dream
Five for the Symbol (stories)
All Visitors Ashore
The Death of the Body
Sister Hollywood
The End of the Century at
    the End of the World
The Singing Whakapapa
Villa Vittoria
The Blind Blonde with Candles
    in her Hair (stories)
Talking about O'Dwyer
The Secret History of Modernism
Mansfield
My Name Was Judas
Risk
The Name on the Door is
    Not Mine (stories)
The Necessary Angel

MEMOIR

South-West of Eden:
    A Memoir 1932–1956
You Have a Lot to Lose:
    A Memoir 1956–1986
What You Made of It:
    A Memoir 1987–2020

CRITICISM

The New Poetic
In the Glass Case
Pound, Yeats, Eliot and the
    Modernist Movement
Answering to the Language
The Writer at Work
Kin of Place: Essays on
    20 New Zealand Writers
Book Self: The Reader as Writer
    and the Writer as Critic
Shelf Life: Reviews, Replies
    and Reminiscences

EDITED

Oxford New Zealand Short
    Stories (second series)
Measure for Measure, a Casebook
Letters and Journals of
    Katherine Mansfield
Collected Stories of
    Maurice Duggan
Faber Book of Contemporary
    South Pacific Stories
Werner Forman's New Zealand

IN THE HALF LIGHT OF A DYING DAY
CATULLUS, 2023

C. K. STEAD

AUCKLAND
UNIVERSITY
PRESS

First published 2024
Auckland University Press
University of Auckland
Private Bag 92019
Auckland 1142
New Zealand
www.aucklanduniversitypress.co.nz

ISBN 978 1 77671 145 1

Published with the assistance of Creative New Zealand

A catalogue record for this book is available from
the National Library of New Zealand.

Design by Duncan Munro

This book was printed on FSC® certified paper

Printed in China by 1010 Printing International Ltd

Catullus poems first appeared in my 1979 collection, *Walking Westward*, and continued to occur at intervals through *Geographies* (1982), *Straw into Gold* (1997) and more or less vanished after *Dog* (2002). Though mine were not translations so much as 'versions in the manner of', there were derived elements, and Catullus's Lesbia became my Clodia – the name of the person on whom his Lesbia is believed to have been based. So the present sequence begins with 'The Clodian Songbook (continued)' but soon introduces the new figure of Kezia (pronounced Key-zya), a name borrowed from Katherine Mansfield who used it for the child, based it seems on herself, in her stories of the Burnell (i.e. Beauchamp) family.

I need to thank my old friend and fellow poet Alan Roddick for watching over this collection as it was emerging and for constantly reviewing it for me and commenting.

In 2014 I was interviewed about my Catullus poems by Dr Maxine Lewis, lecturer in Classics at the University of Auckland, and that interview appeared in my collection, *Shelf Life: Reviews, Replies and Reminiscences* (2016, pp. 287–91).

All the poems in this collection were written during 2023 apart from the first, 'Invocation', written long ago and intended as the opening poem of a new sequence which was never written. It made a first public appearance in the *Times Literary Supplement*, 8 December 2023.

I think this collection might be read as a single work of fiction.

C. K. S.

CONTENTS

Two: Catullus and Kezia

I THE CLODIAN SONGBOOK [CONTINUED]

INVOCATION

Suburb or Sabine farm, not all our hard work
alters, though it orders, as best it can
your rhythms that answer in feather, fin and flower
motions of sun and moon. Look where tides
advancing under the causeway flush the Bay.
Sun silvers the ferns, domestic grass
pricks up to greet the mower, and my timber house
creaks on its jacks. That once I crossed
the rust-red river, heard steel speak and saw
scavengers wait on the dying; that I command
at peace diagrams of dissolving stars
or proceed white-coated against the militant Crab –
such purpose commends itself. But blood must keep
even as Caesar's your lyric measure precisely
or lose itself among the abstract spaces
where no bird builds, nor predator patrols
the sandy shallows,
nor sap rises to inform a tree.

HISTORY

Great Caesar forgave you

                      Catullus

              or seemed to

for those couplets in which you said

        you weren't interested in pleasing

his Greatness

           nor in knowing

what colour his hair would have been

                had he had any

      which might have given more offence

than your jolly scatological stabs

about his taste for boys' backsides

                and the cunts

of his generals' wives –

            forgave, and

           even invited you

to dinner,

accepting your 'grovelling

              (as Licinius

your salty friend described it)

           apology',

      praised the eloquence of your

toast to his victories

congratulated you

on the 'wayward beauty' of your mistress

               Clodia

the wife (as he mentioned
                    so you'd know he knew)
of Quintus Caecilius
                    governor of Cisalpine Gaul.

When he named his favourite poets
                    you didn't sneer,
said only that moralising
                    was 'not your thing'
'And indeed why would it be?'
                    your host remarked
                    with a smile you found
                              profound-   5
ly disconcerting.

He had been your father's friend,
had awarded a medal
                    to your hero brother
who died in his service –
and hadn't he so long ago
                    given you as his friend's
dearest and cleverest little boy
                    the gift of toy soldiers?

A lovely occasion!

establishing peace

forgiveness

and ahead for you Catullus

what waited

but feats in battle and surely

some marvellous posting

in the provinces

followed by favour in Rome?

So why my friend

were you never heard of again?

Did you get home that night

or die

knifed in an alley

by one or two of his minions?

Caesar would soon die, it's true

nine times stabbed

in the Curia of Pompey

on the Ides of March

but at least he would be mourned

written about

his victories celebrated

while for you, Catullus

nothing

only a single rumour
that the dying Emperor Julian
when the spear-wound in his side
opened
and blood gushed forth
was heard to murmur one of your poems

and after
nothing
and again nothing
        except
        until
                from the silence of the grave
and with the passage of so many centuries
            your words and your wit would
                find their way home.

THE FARM

Remember
Catullus
the farm up north
and the three women
the one who was housewife
the one who milked the herd
and one the entertainer
who loved and was loved by
the boy who sang on horseback
and trapped rabbits for the pot and
fished for eels.

Their men were away with Caesar
conquering Gaul
and you were that boy
chopping wood for the range
loving the herd smell
the working dogs
the konaki
that took cream to the gate,
and deep in bush
the sacred grove
with its little waterfall
and subsequent clear pool
where small fish hung like stars
in a secret sky.

8

And then at night
lantern light
around the big kitchen table
the women talking
teasing you Catullus
pretending you were their man
until
candles at brass bed time
and moreporks calling
magic/mysterious
out of the deep, unspeaking
dark.

LICINIUS
[REMEMBERING KEVIN]

Licinius, clubable as you were not
Catullus, liked forms but was indifferent
to Sappho's syllabic count – preferring wine
      and the company

of those boozy Good Old Boys he met for lunch.
So when he died before you there were protests
to the gods who had taken him too early
      and left the sober

Catullus, it seemed, untouched. But in his will
he left to his clever friend a self-portrait,
himself in a yellow hat, asking only
      that when your time came

you would bring him, wherever fate determined
your ghosts might at last convene, your best bottle
of that Te Mata red favoured by you both
      and your newest verse.

So your good friend Licinius calls to you
feelingly across the dark river of death
to say it was art he loved, and poetry
      but not without wine.

10

ODI ET AMO

                              Clodia
                   one of a number
but the first
and still in the world.
                              Beautiful?
                   Then for sure but now
time-worn/time-
wasted
              like her once-and-only
her never-forever
Catullus
         who put her on a pedestal
took her to heart
                            lived for/
                       would have
died for
her
and wrote her into
                   with utter devotion
                   his double margins
                   his eloquent gutters
to live there how
                   now-or-never
long?

'I love and I loathe'
how is that done she asked
                    as she tightened
the screws
          marrying that Cisalpine
Senator
known for knowing
              the meaning of money
and of meanness.

Later

too much later
as the hearse carted Quintus away
                    she embraced you
Catullus
remember?
          You had to turn her about
to watch it depart
                    so she would seem
the proper
widow she was
                    seeing him off
weeping (not sweeping) him
                              away.

Salute, Clodia, our poet of love's
dear one,
dear once –
        did he mean it that day
in his thoughts to send you
with Quintus
for ever into the fire?

HEMI

Hemi
shaggy and barefoot
he was your Diogenes
full of contempt for your wants and your wages
and with a wisdom not all his own –
traditional, Catholic
not entirely to be sneezed at
but for Catullus
retrograde
masculist
at once flashy and necromantic
belonging to a past
best left behind.

When he came to your office
Catullus
asking for 'bread, man'
there was always an embrace
unwelcome as the hippie talk
to one who came (as he did too)
from a generation of men
who did not hug
considered it 'American',
an affectation
and subtly, unmistakably
a reproach.

He was welcome to the 'bread, man'
but it was his dear deserted wife
who was heard to ask
'Why this dressing up
Jim
this pretence at poverty
when you have good shoes in the closet at home
and one or two
suitable suits?'

Hemi/Jim/James K
such a poet you were
so eloquent and at ease
in your chats with God
to whom you dedicated your piety and rags
the lice in your beard
your acts of self-flagellation
the girls you fucked and most of all
your memories of the South.

Catullus envied your fluency
Jim
but thought you might have put it
to better use.

TIME

Catullus
your poet neighbour
Nick and his old friend Mike
have been asking themselves whether Time
could have died in our time.
It would mean that God was dead
and we would be going on
at the speed of light
in a universe of physics and maths
planetary systems
and light years,
of infinity
and $E = mc^2$.
It seemed a thought that might have come
from one of those brainy chaps
Einstein,
or even Wittgenstein
or maybe from the Muse of poetry
to Keats
knowing he'd soon be dead.
Kia ora Nick and Mike
Catullus salutes you.

COMPASSION

How far into the meal
at Caesar's table
were you Catullus
when he told you that story
about what he called
compassion?
He'd been captured by pirates
and warned them that crucifixion
would be their punishment,
and, rescued,
felt he must keep his word,
but when they were up
nailed to their crosses
he'd had their throats cut
to speed the process.
You wondered were you meant to understand it
as a warning
or was it only
the sociable dictator's
after-dinner chat?

CREATIVE WRITING CLASS?

It was long ago
Catullus
you complained
with uncommon eloquence
that your friend Rufus
who had seemed to love you
had betrayed you, spoken against you
poisoned your name.
You were young and needed to learn
that bitter verses
however well-turned
however clever the poet
just the cause and
elevated the Muse
still leave a bad taste.
Lighten it Catullus –
remember
the gift of happiness
can't be matched.
You don't have to forgive Rufus
but smile at least for your readers,
be kind to them.

UNCERTAINTY

Remember, Catullus
when you were young
and in love with Clodia
sitting with friends
around the table under a green screen of vines
looking out on that bluest of seas
enjoying good wine and witty gossip
you wondered
who among us might have been fucking whom
sure of nothing
but the grammar
and even of that
less than certain.

LANGUAGE

Clodia wondered whether when you said,
                                    Catullus,
                    that you couldn't say
                you hadn't loved your Briton
it meant you had;
                    and when you called her Anglia
                        you really meant Angel
or on the other hand maybe
a cheap little Runabout.
                    She told you once she was Māori
and entertained you with snatches of te reo
                        caught from the air waves:
                            'Koinā ngā pūrongo hākinakina'
for example
or just 'Mā te wā'.
                    In a restaurant she asked the waiter
                            'E whai ake nei?'
and he surprised her with
                            'That's up to you, Madame.
Would you like to see the menu for desserts?'
or so she told you.
                    She was with Quintus of course
                who could afford a restaurant with waiters
                            calling customers Sir
and Madame
and who told her 'dessert' was 'non-U' –
                    the right word was 'pudding'.

Another time she told you she was Jewish
                          'but on Daddy's side
so it doesn't count.'
                          Was it then she gave you
a blast of German
in which you thought you heard
                          'Das ist die Kreide' and then
'die Kreide ist weiß'
                          suggesting the classroom –
or was it about race
and colour?
          There was a lot of French between you;
that was when you talked of running away
to Paris together –
but mostly it was the language of love
                          in which you both were fluent
in person and on the page
O faithless ones!

WORLD'S END

In your big bossy Green-tone
                              Catullus
you tell us humanity's doomed
but you don't quite mean it
                         do you?
        It's a serious warning
        but I think I know what you think,
that the self-harm we do
        will be enormous, immeasurable –
wars, atomic bombs and oil spills
floods, fires and famine
                nuclear winters and pandemics
species wipeouts and
                        unstoppable migrations –
all our own fault
                        bringing surely
                        death to half the race
or (ridiculous even to guess)
                        more than half?
                and yet we'll survive –
is what you believe, my Optimist
we humans having, along with our
                        matchless stupidity,
such courage
resourcefulness, sheer ingenuity
and inventiveness,

we can recognise what we do
even as we do it
and slowly make things right.
No comfort to the dead and dying
while it's happening
but a kind of reassurance
for those able to look beyond
the many more millions
of centuries left to us
until the universe itself bids us goodbye
and without our assistance
enforces world's end.

C. M. T.

It was your captain Cato
Catullus
said you did well

                not to let lust fester.
He'd seen you coming from the brothel
        where your love was working off
her student loan;
    but seeing you there yet again he warned
'Two nights in succession, my boy –

             is she your Cleopatra?'
meaning to remind you of our general
Mark Antony

              who let lust rule his roost
              and rust his armour
        and lost that battle with Augustus.
'Honour is not found in bed'

             he thundered
disturbing the peace of Lupanar
and setting the dogs barking

        'but in battle and in blood';
then gave you at Parade-ground pitch
lines from Horace about hard campaigning
against the Parthian enemy.

          Thanks Captain Cato
        Catullus will keep it in mind
while alas the ZCl of his heart's
still tuned to Venus.

THE GOOD MAN IN LOVE

Remember Catullus how you told the gods
you were a good man, honest
who when you spoke of your feelings for her
and promised fidelity, kindness, enduring love
it was all true
whereas she (you droned on)
Clodia
was untruthful, unfaithful, and unworthy of
all you offered.
So you grumbled and grovelled
begging them to give you strength
to shake off this blackest of diseases
that bound you to her wheel of fire.
If their Highnesses could find for you
compassion, you told them
and rescue you from love
you would go on for life
being this good man so plain to their godly eyes
and would die as you had lived
their servant
a man at peace with himself
and with the world
no longer the tormented wretch
now begging for their help.
Often it seemed they had granted your prayer
so that in old age
Venus was leaving you alone.

So why in these last of your years
herself long dead
do you think of her still
and try to contrive a meeting:
'Just one' you whine and plead
to the patch-eyed boatman who's not listening
as he sculls you across the Black River
where you've dreamed she will be waiting.

EGO

Knowing your own insignificance
Catullus
your unnoticeable non-existence
among the cloud showers
of stars
and the chaos
of black holes forming and collapsing,
still and nonetheless
you hope to be heard
to make yourself visible
to shout what you know
into the clamour of the Big Bang
and the infinite eternal Silence
of big Him.
No need for this effort my friend,
leave it to the lesser gods
those self-appointed
snappers at your heels
to make known
to no one
and for ever
your failure to make yourself
known.
Count on it my poet of love
you haven't done enough harm
to deserve a lll call up there

and not enough good
even for a place below the salt
at the on-going
eternal table.
They won't fail you
Catullus:
their promises of offering
a 'No comment' on your name
or just '*Who?*'
are always kept.

IANUS

Ianus
your sister said you were a bully
and when news came you were killed in battle
in faraway Bithynia,
refused to weep.
Catullus shed tears for you both,
and here he is at your grave
travel-weary
weeping again, weeping still,
sorry for himself, sorry especially
for you his good mate
dear friend
victim of that argumentative god
Field Marshal Mars
with his silly headgear and his
noseless truculent face
who pushed you into service
in another of his pointless wars.
So Catullus brings you what custom requires
in tribute and salutation
his forever and forever
never to be unsaid
never forgotten
brother
hail and farewell.

II CATULLUS AND KEZIA

HOME

You ask, friend Filius
where Catullus and Kezia
are living now:
truth is they're still in the lovely gully
you've heard them praise so often
that shelters them and runs on down to a bay
where seabirds gather
to feed and make ready
for annual migrations over land and ocean,
journeys your friends
used to replicate
by the miracle of Air New Zealand –
and still in the 'kit-set' house they built around them
making it up
as their family grew.
But no more travel for them
and though they remember so fondly
and weep for times spent
in your villa by that bluest of all seas
old age has taught them
to love what they have
this green enclave where flowers and fruit flourish,
where tūī and blackbird,
pigeon, sparrow and thrush
build
and teach their young to fly,

33

while at high tide
the kingfish come close inshore
to hunt for flounder.
Even the recent floods swept right on by
and left them dry –
a rhyme bestowed by the local deity
or mysterious Chance
to whom Catullus can offer
nothing by way of gratitude
but his imperfect verses.
'Thank you, my mysterious friend,'
he says,

and says it again
'Thank you'.

LANGUAGE AGAIN

                        Watching *Succession* with you
Kezia
Catullus remembers so far back when
                scarcely adults you two made love
in your grandpa's bed or among the pines
                        at Waikumete
and pretended
you might number your 'kisses'
                against sand grains at Ahipara
or the show of stars you saw over his shoulder
on your back on the golf course there
                        and asked
how many it would take
to slake a thirst, abate a hunger . . .

reflecting now
not disapproving but perhaps astonished
                what a measure of time passing
usage can be
where 'fuckn' is the adjective of choice tumbling
from the pretty lips of top 'world famous' actors
or those who write their lines.
        It's the language of your Catullus, Kezia
                of the gutter and of the stars
and explains why the goddess Diana
too fine-grained and finicky

     for the reality you mostly enjoy,
disapproving of
not just his deeds with you
    but his world-soiled words,
       hides herself
and will not listen
or let you see her face.

MODERN MIRACLES

Your London daughter
Kezia
believes she hears something
in your conversation
by phone across half a world
and in your breathing
and googles it
soon enough to earn you
a diagnosis and a course
of radiotherapy.
She's here so soon
(Business Class)
that our forebears
watching (let's say) from Beyond
gasp and admire –
such good fortune,
so much time for travels and goodbyes
than was ever theirs!
But for the rescue,
the cure?
Probably not.
That's a further,
a future
too far dimension.

FREE WILL?

Kezia grasps your wrist
Catullus
and thanks you for staying at her side.
Anyone overhearing
might think she means now,
nursing her in her illness,
but you know she means a lifetime
your three score years and ten
of being together.
You tell her leaving was never in your thoughts
and quote those old lines of yours
she knows so well
about the hungry dog in this iron time.
'No', she insists grasping your wrist
even more firmly.
'It was a choice.'

JUST LOOKING

Together, C and K
you look at,
marvel at,
Marti's magic –
her pic of you both young
the inherited
Irish look
yours Catholic Catullus
Kezia's Prot
but both neutral
open
cheerful/indifferent
without the faith,
the enmity and
the menace –
two *tabulae rasae*
waiting for the world
to imprint
something, anything
on the beautiful nothings
of then.
You remind her of her joking uncles'
explanation for her 'Māori look' –
their sister's
'pā-sneaking'.

You've just watched a British pic
with Helen Mirren
that ends with a man coming out of jail
to a chorus of 'Jerusalem'
and you sing it, remember
Catullus
full voice
as you prepare to sleep.

THE PANIC

You've been missed of late
Kezia
in the street
and down at the Bay.
When people ask
Catullus tells them you've not been well
and they wish you all the best.
In a panic he asks himself
what's in the offing?
Could Kezia die?
What would he do with himself
with your 'things',
your favourite shirts and sweaters,
your scents and your secrets?
He can't think
but thinks he knows
he'd keep them as they are,
untouched, unchanged.
They are you, Kezia
his love,
he'll live with them
for ever.
He'll die with them.

READING

Kezia always out-read you
Catullus
two books to one – or more.
Many of yours were poetry
fewer words, but more
re-readings,
nuttings out
puzzling over.
It was never a competition
but collaboration
each adding to the other's store
as in Pound's
Ezraversity
or 14 Esmonde Road
under Sargeson's guidance.
Only in these last months
she's said she finds it tiring
while you,
90 and challenged by sleep,
are already nodding
over your Paradise Lost.
Didn't you two begin
as librarian and student
and don't you seem
to be exiting
by the same doors?

PAIN

After that battle-wound
Catullus
you spoke about the pain
seldom or never
but lived with it;
no Coriolanus display of scars
to earn yourself a place in our hearts
or in the Senate
but a silence as if the hurt had been too deep
ever to be touched upon
for fear of return,
for fear of hatred and rage,
a dream of a memory
was it?
Only you can say, my twin.
But not the pain of another,
your dearest Kezia
in the claws of the Crab
in the long night
and all the way until morning;
no one to blame for this and no place for rage
as you rub her back to ease it
right hand first
then change for respite left,
ribcage, spine, the shoulder-blade and shoulder
she panting, shivering, sweating
seeming so small so shrunken and depleted
and still so loved.

The gods
unhelpful as always
silent, indifferent
are keeping tight about it
doing nothing except
to render you useless
Catullus
with only your box of words to play with
and no new word for despair.

THE OTHER DOOR

As Kezia grows weaker
Catullus
she can't sit up with you following
episode by episode
Succession
with its narrative of the Roy siblings
competing to inherit
the family business,
but waits to hear from you
when you bring it to bed
the story so far.
So you give her in turn
the ups and down
of Connor and Shiv
Roman and Kendall
as they rise and fall
while the old man plays them
like the game fish they are
never settling the matter.
Each night
Kezia's attention grows fainter
wanting to know the end
but closer always to sleep,
to the big sleep.

Your telling is vivid
Catullus
but not enough
to keep her listening
when it is death that's knocking
at the other door.

THE SIGNAL

Remember Catullus
your first flat together
on the beach at Takapuna
that looked out across the Hauraki Gulf
to Rangitoto
and how
scared of the dark
Kezia would ask you to come with her at night
across the little courtyard
to the loo you shared
with Hazel and Felix?
Ailing now and
wanting your support
to help her to one of the two loos
you share with no one
she whispers 'Takapuna'
and you take her hand
into the dark.

ALWAYS

Not able to enjoy her meals
she keeps trying to please you
Catullus,
one night a success
and hope for better,
the next impossible.
Day by day she seems to shrink
but she can still be helped by you
to the end of the street
to chat to the neighbour Keith
with his dog Winstone
and watch with them
the tide arrive and depart
over the mud-flats.
Sun or showers it doesn't matter
for Kezia
it's the same
always a miracle.

SORRY

Kezia is dead
Catullus
you know that and need to know.
You had given the drug to ease the pain
and were glad to see her sleep
and climbed in beside her
and slept
and woke was there a reason
missing the sound of her breathing
the tiny lung whistle
the effort.
She was on her side
right hand forward and spread
as if reaching for something
for another breath
just one
even the last.
You kissed her cheek
Catullus
and told her you were sorry
and wept.
She would have wept to see you weeping
but could not
did not know they were your tears
falling on her face
did not know anything
anymore
who had known so much.

When you dialled 111
they asked was she cold in a warm room
(she was)
was she stiff
(she was not, you could move her fingers).
Waiting for them
you went back and back to her
and kissed her brow and her cheek
and closed her eyes
and ran your fingers through her damp hair
and told her how sorry you were
that you had not saved her
protected her from the pain
and from the death, sorry
that you had slept
when she was dying,
yourself still
like a fool, like an idiot
like one who has lost his mind
rambling pointlessly on
sobbing that you were
sorry.

THE SCIENCE

... tells us
that after the heart stops
and we are technically dead
the brain lives a while
perhaps many minutes
even an hour

no longer in pain
but in some 'near death'
'passing over' moment
of our own invention
possibly beautiful
symbolic
mystical –

a departing ship full-sail,
a full choir singing 'Jerusalem'
as a man emerges from jail,
Charon's wherry on the Black River ...

Must Catullus believe this
Kezia?
He shrinks from it
fears it
and yet

asks himself
why?

NOT YET?

Wanting to die
Catullus
and ready to relax into death
as into a soft bed
or a warm bath
you are called back to life
by an idea
for this one more
small
last poem.
Is it the Muse calls you
or just the will to live
in weak disguise?

THE SILENCE

In the undertaker's parlour
today Catullus
you wore your new hearing aids
to listen
beside finely refurbished Kezia
to the Silence.
She lay there
in her plain wood coffin
no more serious than you
but focussed
wearing that dark grey shirt we'd chosen,
red-brown silk scarf,
black trousers and black-shined shoes
so small they touched the heart.
Not a pin was dropped,
not a tear fell:
you and she Catullus
were elsewhere, otherwhere
nowhere.

53

GALLIA

These days without you Kezia
Catullus goes back to your summers together
in Gallia
and your walks each morning
from the village
through cornfields and vineyards
where cicadas sing
to their silent wives,
through woods past an ancient mill
for coffee in that town from which
great Augustus had tapped an underground source
of purest water
and ran it by a triple aqueduct
le Pont du Gard
to supply his garrison at Nîmes –
you two
rehearsing as you walked
secrets and future plans.
Lacking a future now
Catullus walks with you again
Kezia
glad of those summers,
inventing or rediscovering
conversations
about Catholic Gallia
where pines sigh their prayers
a poplar chatters its confession

and in April red poppies hide
like sins in a wheatfield –
but before the Popes
you remind yourselves,
came the Caesars
including the greatest
whose channel still runs on
as if for ever
past village and through vineyard
and on to his garrison
at Nîmes.

OSLO

You always thought of Oslo as Solo
and Paris as Pairs
so your bed with Kezia
Catullus
was Paris
Saint Sulpice, the Latin Quarter
the Seine
two singles pushed together
making just one of you
with double sheets and blankets
and double bedcover
in blue.
Now it will be single
bed, sheets, blankets, but the same
blue cover disguising
that where you have arrived
in truth mein Doppelgänger
is Oslo.

8/9/2023

Even without your new aids
Catullus
at 6 a.m. you hear the first bird-call
cheerful, but to you
melancholy
because solo
(Oslo).

You've seen new blossom
starting
(startling)
white
on the plum tree
and buds on the vine.
Today they give you a new hip.
Kia kaha!

THE RACE

Why did your dream
Catullus
remember being puzzled
racing big Daddy Death
over the sands of Palm Beach
that your four-year-old scamper
your quick-as-lightning flicker
could not out-pace
his slow loping
inevitable
stride?

LAST

Last night
in the dark of a hospital bed
Catullus
you quoted
faint but distinct
audible to your own
un-aided
ears
and to the ghost at your side
John Donne's
'Nocturnal upon
St Lucy's Day'
with its iterations
of nothing
and nothingness
and its
resolute

'but I am
none
nor will my sun
renew.'

HOME AGAIN

Mae
the Chinese cleaning lady
opens arms wide
to give you a hug
Catullus
and tells you
Kezia wants you to live
and the cat Nico
needs you
and you find yourself
wanting to believe her.

THE PLUM TREE

Few bees this year
in the windy spring
but there must have been some
or maybe it was the white-eyes
(pihipihi)
were doing the mahi
when you were dying
Kezia
and now
the small enamel green bullets
that will be round and red by Christmas
are arriving
on the tree outside your kitchen.
Wearing his new
MedicAlert
Catullus loiters
in what you called his Lockwood 'office'
among the scatter
of poems and books
the abandoned drafts and cuttings
hoping like Wilkins Micawber
that something will turn up
and comes upon only
a very thin poem
by W. C. Williams
about an old lady
eating plums.

They taste good to her
the poet says
and repeats it:
they taste good to her.

A BEGINNING

Do you remember
Kezia
it was 17 October
1962
Catullus's birthday
when the Cuban Missile
Crisis began
and on that day
mysteriously
you decided
it was time to have children.
A year later he would bring you the news
that our Caesar had been
assassinated and,
your first born at your breast,
you would shed a tear
your blessing on the tiny brow.
It seemed
or seems at this distance
the start of a new decade
two decades
of the Beatles and the bombings
and an obsession
his and yours
with that obscene
evil
unnecessary war.

NOW

Now you're solo in the night
Catullus
you can practise singing
ballads
and the popular songs of your youth
'True Love', 'Blue Smoke'
without disturbing anyone
but the passing or resident ghost
who sometimes you suspect
laughs
not scornfully but with affection
when you lose the note.

TALKING TO THE CAT

To Nico Catullus tries to speak only
Māori
which has been recommended
as a way of learning te reo.
Nico replies volubly
(he was always a talkative cat)
in his own first language
almost certainly
Siamese.
When the nights are cold
he occupies your space
Kezia
and Catullus sometimes half-wakes
to the sensation
of a small rough tongue
licking his hand.
It's Nico's way of saying
'I know you miss her Catullus.
So do I.'

FOR WE

How can Catullus pretend
he didn't enjoy this morning
though the electric kettle leaked
on his breakfast
and down at the Bay
the tide came over the path
wetting his walkers?
Can he acknowledge this Kezia
without losing you
his dearest
his for everest friend
though you were not there
(were you?)
to share
the mini dramas
and the jokes with which
he entertained himself?
Who was the rapper said
'I'm in it for we'
meaning Black
his community of colour?
Today Catullus says it
of you and himself
Kezia:
'I'm in it for we.'

'NOW MORE THAN EVER SEEMS IT RICH...'

Last night Kezia
Catullus called up
his ever-ready Keats
nightingale ode
and remembered how
in the same bed
when you were dying
you'd asked for the same poem
and he'd had to stop
at the sixth stanza
because you were weeping
at those lines that displayed
so poignantly
how the Muse could call forth
out of the nowhere
of a poet's inner self
words so precisely placed
on the cliff-edge between
beauty and death
that poet and reader alike
must pause and weep.

THE GOOD LIFE

Remember how you two laughed
Kezia
at Wittgenstein's formula
for good living?
'It doesn't matter what you eat
so long as it's always the same.'
Lacking you to cook for
or to cook for him,
Catullus claims
he's getting closer
to the philosopher's ideal
and takes up that line again
that he can only cook
'for we,
never for me';
so lunch has to be what's over
from the too much of
the night before;
but he can still sometimes rise to
one of your favourites
Kezia
like that special pasta
with eggplant, red onion, capsicum
and a garlic-tomato sauce,
which he serves with a glass of red
and raises it to that image of you two
looking good together,
like a well-judged half-rhyme
with a bowl of grapes on the table.

Those were the days
when your vine flourished
after the plums were done
and you'd come to a late agreement
with thrush and blackbird
that your fruit was their fruit
and had to be shared.

TRUE LOVE

In your dream, Catullus
you were swimming at Kohi
and reached the yellow buoy
which had lately been
beyond your powers.
You were elated
and returning on your back
enjoying those whitest of white fleeces
against that bluest of blue
summer skies
you sang to yourself
'True love'
remembering Grace Kelly
singing
with pipe-smoking Bing.
So you came ashore
ready to boast –
but the beach was empty,
and where were your clothes?
'Kezia will have them' you told yourself –
and woke . . .

MADNESS?

Catullus thanks 'God'
that he and Kezia
were never sucked down
into the Netherwhere
of conspiracy theorists
and anti-vaxxers
or he might have been persuaded
to see those clouds he studies
when swimming on his back
not as Nature's
accidental/incidental
miraculous
works of art,
but as gunships in a war,
emitters of invisible rays
deployed by a government
or some other secret agent
hell-bent on power and control.
What should we trust, he asks
in the world of the internet
that seems so near, offering
such ease of access
and so much of it so nearly
insane?
Night after night since your funeral
Kezia
he has played the Wagner cycle
you'd banned at bedtime

himself imagining
that five-footer (Keats's height)
in the velvet jacket and the satin collars
at work at his clavier
where Wotan and Brünnhilde,
Sieglinde and Siegfried,
and the giants, and the dwarfs
the Rhinemaidens, and the Ring itself
were imagined to life
and to such song,
such frantic
ravishing
incomparable
song.

THE WOUND

You know, Catullus
Kezia never believed
you'd stopped loving Clodia
nor thought those incandescent poems
you wrote about her
were true or deserved.
Clodia she quite admired
as 'a nice woman,
not clever, but civilised,
refined, fluent in French
and a good mother;
but married
(her misfortune)
to money.'
So much you had written
Catullus
about Clodia
Kezia read with amusement
and many grains of salt.
They were poems, she said
(becoming for a moment
the literary critic)
that had to be written
because of your deplorable
romantic ego
and the wound it had sustained.

THE STORY?

Here Kezia
you and he are fictions
Romanised for the convenience
of the one (another fiction)
who calls himself
Catullus;
but as you've come, through him,
to know yourselves
you've seemed to be living out the end
of the twentieth Christian century
the one in which the folk who'd been taught
to write by hand
began to unlearn that skill
finding ways to make machines
do it for them
while music became electronic
poetry wayward
and language lawless.
So much 'becoming'
by which you and he together
have recognised the passing of time
and the loss of the cheerfully compliant
child-self
in the complaining
olding adult.

At your funeral
Kezia
you were described as
radical, outspoken
not because
you two differed in what you espoused
but because you were the frank one,
colourful, memorable.
Recently a friend sent
pics of you arm-in-arm.
What a beautiful
radical grandma
you were, Kezia
and how Catullus misses that bold talk
those strong convictions
that remembering and rational mind
to whose affable ghost
he sometimes sings in the night.

THE PUZZLE

When you were dying Kezia
the dreams of Catullus
took him back
south-west of Eden
to scoria Auckland
with veggie gardens and chooks
and trams (how he'd loved them)
and ferries.
Night after night he'd go
'into town' meaning 'town'
as it had been –
no Harbour Bridge, no tunnels or Sky Tower

but those commercial
street photographers
catching us all
in black-and-white
jackets and ties,
hats and (ladies) gloves,
that world so full of
a faraway war
and here at home
full of proprieties and restraint
and secrets.
After what the Bible deems
a life-span
with you his good companion
he thought he wanted to die

so what was taking him back
so vividly
to his beginnings
saying to the death-wish
'Soon perhaps
but not yet.'
Could there have been something
still to be revealed,
something 'unhousel'd, disappointed,
unaneal'd'?

CATULLUS DEMONSTRATES A VULGAR TASTE

Tonight Kezia
Catullus watched on Sky
that childhood favourite
Singin' in the Rain
with Gene Kelly and Debbie Reynolds
and went to bed so elated
he couldn't put on
the Beethoven Quartet he had ready.
Such grandeur
would have seemed a travesty,
would have wrecked those
O-so-singable tunes,
the marvellous sense of movement
and the timing
that had set his inner man
dancing.
So he went to sleep remembering,
hoping to dream of
his loving Nana
who night after night
when Hollywood called her
(Fred Astaire and Ginger Rogers
especially)
would walk into town
to watch the same movie
and come home singing.
It's in the genes
Kezia
unavoidable, irresistible, basic.

A BUTTON

Ironing a blue shirt
Kezia
the one you'd especially admired,
Catullus came on a button
that didn't match the rest.
His welling
irrepressible sadness
at that moment
had nothing to do with
ironing or shirts
nor with sewing and mending
and household
chores
but with this cruel reminder
that you were gone
and would not be back.

FIRST LIGHT

Kezia's funeral
Catullus
was yours too
no need for another.
Fine weather forecast
and an early tide
you are up at first light
to swim at Kohi
remembering days
when Kezia swam with you there
to the yellow buoy
in a sea that looked like glass
and felt like silk
and the vast beautiful harbour
under the enigma
of Rangitoto
felt like forever.

AFTER DEATH

If it's true that what you believe
determines where you go
you are Nowhere now
Kezia
and Catullus is to follow.
But how does he know
you're not anchored
in Hawaiki watching
with your 'pā-sneaking' mum
and her jokey brothers
the sunset mirrored in the bay
while for himself there waits
a Norse cloud
in a Wagnerian twilight
with Valkyries overhead
and in the basement
dwarfs banging pots and pans
with threatening precision.
'You will know when you get there'
wrote our brilliant and strangely pertinent
poet friend
thinking no doubt of Lone Kauri Road
down to that drumming sea
in the half light of a dying day.